Things Jesus Never Said

John Moore

DEDICATION

I'd like to dedicate this to my loyal subjects, the citizens of Norway. Also to my lovely wife and kids, who I love more than bacon. To my top secret instructors in the arts of the shadow warrior. To the crew of my ship – arrrgggggghh.

THINGS JESUS NEVER SAID

My birthday? I dunno, chop down some trees and drag them indoors.

Dude, I can totally surf boardless.

Megachurches and pastors with private jets? Sounds legit.

Hey, what are you guys doing for Easter break?

The Bible's pretty clear on idol worship, but can you throw some crosses up everywhere?

I know I said a lot of stuff about love, but you should hate people who are different from you.

Screw starving kids, I am here to determine the outcomes of football games.

In the future, when people paint pictures of me, I hope they make me white.

I don't like gay people, which is why I wear a dress and hang around with men.

YOLO!

Mel Gibson is EXACTLY what I had in mind.

Blessed are the beatmakers, now lay down that funky drum solo.

When I rise from the dead, we should totally celebrate with a Germanic pagan fertility festival.

Do unto others … wait, Buddha said that first? What the heck, nobody will know. It's not like they're writing this shit down.

It's totally OK to make anything up you want and say that it's what I would have wanted.

All 41,000 sects of Christianity are right.

Since the only way to get into heaven is through me, that pretty much screws everyone who has ever lived up until now.

Always wipe front to back.

If anything good happens, be sure to give me credit.

As a prank, we should totally write down some bronze-age superstitions and say they're the word of god.

You guys realize I'm Jewish, right?

You can kill people and stuff but, if you say some magic words, we're OK.

After I ascend to heaven, I'll let people know I'm still watching by putting pictures of myself in their toast.

When a doctor with a decade of medical training saves somebody's life, say it was a miracle.

My father is omnipotent and loving,
now I'm off to be tortured to death.

God doesn't love your baby until you sprinkle water on it and say the magic words.

God loves all creatures great and small, but not people who don't go to your church.

The Bible says slavery is OK, so I guess – go ahead.

I wonder how long I can chill upstairs and people will still think I'm coming back.

John Moore

Water into wine… let's see
Copperfield do that!

God is the omnipotent, omniscient, and omnipresent creator of the entire universe, and it's really east to offend him.

Seriously, masturbate all you want.

Dinosaurs? Never heard of them.

Please don't start a war over any of this.

Even I can't bring Firefly back.

I'm not really into politics.

Judge not … aw, who am I kidding? Judge away!

Your 97th great-grandmother ate some fruit and that's why you menstruate.

For hundreds of years I will inspire people to write some of the greatest music the world has ever heard. In the 20th century and beyond, religious music is going to suck.

Oatmeal raisin cookies are an abomination. It's chocolate chip or nothing.

God is everywhere, but you have to go to a special building once a week and give the guy in the robes money.

God answers all prayers. No, not out loud. That would be crazy.

Magic and witchcraft are evil, now have some of this magic wine and bread.

Even though the English language wouldn't be invented for well over a thousand years, the King James Bible is a word for word dictation of what I actually said.

When I go down a water-slide,
BOOM, whole pool full of holey
water.

Even though God created the whole universe from nothing, he still needs your money.

For millennia, mankind has worshipped thousands of gods. But I'm the real one, I promise.

For my next miracle, watch me pull this rabbit out of my hat.

Let he who is without sin cast the first stone. You there! Put that down!

Satan's best trick was fossils.

Love thy enemy, unless he or she is into anal.

Compared to my Mom, your Mom's a whore.

In my father's house there are many rooms. I can't find the remote.

Render unto Caesar the things that are Caesar's. Don't forget to return his lawnmower.

If you confess to a priest who diddles boys, it doesn't count.

After the crucifixion, it whistles when I give high-fives.

If I were around today, you'd all think I was a crazy homeless hippy.

Hey Judas, why don't you leave the tip!

Listen kids, I don't even know what Lucky Charms are or why you'd be after them, and I'm not ratting out the Leprechaun.

Listen, when the whole thing about pork was written, bacon hadn't been invented yet. Go for it.

If socks had been invented, I totally would have worn them with sandals.

ABOUT THE AUTHOR

John Moore is a wicked awesome comedy writer who is also the King of Norway, a pirate, and a ninja. Catch him on Twitter at @johnalogue

www.ingramcontent.com/pod-product-compliance
Lightning Source LLC
Chambersburg PA
CBHW021221020426
42331CB00003B/415